MW01123348

PORTEÑOS TALK

- Understanding the language
of Buenos Aires-

Verónica de la Vega

HÉCTOR DINSMANN EDITOR

Buenos Aires, 2000

Un sincero agradecimiento
a Chris Southworth y Elina Malamud
por sus comentarios y sugerencias
en la elaboración y revisión del libro.

Gracias también a la gran familia AFS
alrededor del mundo.

801-3=00=20=60	Vega, Verónica de la
VEG	Porteños talk: understanding the languaje
	of Buenos Aires - 1ª ed. - Buenos Aires:
	Héctor Dinsmann Editor, 2000
	107 pp.; 20 x 14 cm.
	ISBN 950-98087-0-3
	I. Título - 1. Glosario Inglés-Español

Diseño
Natacha Dinsmann y Aldana Martorell

Impreso en Gráfica Laf S.R.L.,
Loyola 1654, Buenos Aires,
República Argentina,
en junio de 2000.

CONTENTS

1. INTRODUCTION

Dear Visitor :

We are very happy you could come to Buenos Aires, **la reina del Plata** (Queen of the River Plate). We hope you have a great time with us, **los porteños**- the inhabitants of the capital city.

With this book, we would like to introduce you to some aspects of our culture. Particularly, our language and its local variations to the standard Spanish, the **Lunfardo** (slang related to tango tradition) and the modern city jargon.

You will find phrases to meet all situations during your stay : sightseeing, shopping, going places, eating out, and more. We also have included tips on things you should not miss while in **Baires** - those little components of our daily life, and most often the reasons why we love this city and miss it so badly when we are away.

Have you already noticed the pretty art nouveau buildings, the million cafes, the rat race in the **microcentro** (downtown) or the maybe unexpected melting pot the city is? Let's have a little chat! We would love to know all about you.

¡Bienvenido a nuestra casa! (Welcome to our home!)

Verónica de la Vega

2. MAIN FEATURES OF THE RIO DE LA PLATA (RDLP) SPANISH AND SLANG

If you have ever taken Spanish lessons, maybe you remember the second person singular *"tú"* (the familiar or informal "you", as opposed to the more formal **"usted"**)

Well, here we use the form **"vos"** instead of *"tú"* - not to be confused with the person "vosotros", the plural "you" that is used only in Spain (equal to **"ustedes"** in Latin America).

By the same token, all verbs in *the present tense* are conjugated differently for the person vos. Usually, the main difference is in the accent. The last syllable takes a marked stress. And sometimes a vowel is added or omitted. Therefore, if you learned:

"¿Tú dónde trabajas?" (Where do you work?) here becomes : **¿Vos dónde trabajás?**

And, *"¿Cuántos años tienes?"* (How old are you?) becomes : **¿Cuántos años tenés?**

"¿Qué quieres para beber?" (What do you want to drink?), **¿Qué querés para beber?** and so on.
The good news is that the pronoun "your" : tu , remains the same. **¿Cuál es tu nombre?** (What's your name?) or **¿Este es tu asiento?** (Is this your seat?) do not change.

However, the forms *"a ti"* and *"para ti"* (to/for you) become **"a vos"** or **"para vos"**, such as in :

Esto es para vos. (This is for you) and the colloquial **¿A vos te gusta ir a bailar?** (Do you like going dancing?)

Some examples of verbs in the present tense are :

STANDARD SPANISH	RDLP SPANISH	ENGLISH
tú compras	vos comprás	you buy
tú das	vos das	you give
tú dices	vos decís	you say
tú eres	vos sos	you are (definitions)
tú estás	vos estás	you are (temporary states)
a ti te gusta	a vos te gusta	you like
tú hablas	vos hablás	you speak
tú te llamas	vos te llamás	you are called (your name is)
tú miras	vos mirás	you watch
tú puedes	vos podés	you can
tú quieres	vos querés	you like/ want
tu vas	vos vas	you go
tú vienes	vos venís	you come
tú vives	vos vivís	you live

(II)

Imperative forms also change :

"Dame" (Give me) stays the same, but

"Dime" (Tell me) becomes **Decíme**

"Tráeme" (Bring me) : **Traéme**

"Vé" (Go) : **Andá** (vos)

"Escribe" (Write) : **Escribí**

"Siéntate" (Sit down) : **Sentáte**

"Pon" (Put) : **Poné**

"Haz" (Do) : **Hacé** , etc.

(III)

PRONUNCIATION

A) All vowels are pronounced in Spanish.
Roughly there are five vowel sounds :

-a : as in "glass" or "class" (Am. Eng.) and
    "cat" or "mat" (Brit. Eng.)
-e : as in "pet" or "bet".
-i : as in "fee" or "bee"
-o : as in "rob" or "not"
-u : as in "moose" or "goose"

Therefore, in a word like **vacaciones**
(vacations/holidays) all vowels have to be
pronounced.
Something like = [vaacaaceeones].

Follow the reference list!

Also, when a syllable has a written accent, it is stressed. For example, **día** (day), has a stress on the vowel "i".

For those words without a written accent you will find, from now on, a phonetic accent (') to show that the following syllable carries the stress in the word. e.g. ciu'dad (city) carries a stress in the last syllable, "dad". The phonetic accent precedes the syllable.

B) A characteristic very particular to RDLP Spanish is the pronunciation of the consonants "y" and **"ll"**. There are two ways to pronounce them : "sh" as in "she", or "g" as in "George".
Listen to porteños talk and practice!

(IV)

Lun'fardo is the old city slang. Its authentic version is still predominant in the speech of the typical tango lover, usually in his or her 50's and up.
In its origin, Lunfardo was mostly used by the lower classes.

SOME FEATURES

(A) Things are usually called by another name, as you can find in almost all tango lyrics. Some terms have become old-fashioned, however the list below is still *very* popular.
In some cases it becomes difficult to determine whether a word has a Lunfardo origin or just comes from street slang.

LUNFARDO AND STREET SLANG

abom'bado (stupid, nerd)

afa'nar (to steal)   **a'fano** (rip-off)

ato'rrante (1.streetwise 2. bad-intentioned person) also **ato'rranta** (fem. : a slut)

ba'boso/a (someone who falls in love with everybody)

bacán (rich, well-off)

ba'lurdo (problem, mess)

ba'randa (bad smell)

basure'ar (to discrespect or insult)

ba'tir (to squeal, to tell secrets)

be'rreta (low quality, cheap)

bi'orsi (bathroom)
bo'chorno (scandal)

bo'lazo (lie or exaggerated statement)

bo'liche (discotheque, bar, club)

'bondi (bus)

botón (squealer)

bulín (bachelor's apartment)

'busca (jack-of-all-trades)

ca'fiyo (1.pimp. 2.someone who lives on other people's work)

'cana (police)

capicúa (1. to speak in a way that you repeat the first word you said at the end of the sentence : "Tengo 'hambre 'tengo". 2. good luck number with the sequence repeated backwards; such as 404 or 23432)

'capo (someone very respected in a field; genius or wizard)

cara'dura (shameless person)

ca'trera (bed)

ci'ruja (bum)

'coima or co'meta (bribe)

'croto /a (someone with a bad appearance or dressed poorly)

'curda (drinking binge)

chabón (guy, man)

chambón/a (someone who does things fast and carelessly)

chamu'yar (to small talk)   **cha'muyo** or 'verso (small talk)

'changa (a temporary job with a low salary)

'chanta (lier, con artist)

¡che! (hey! ,yo!)

'chorro/a (thief)

chupa'medias (brown-noser)

'chusma (gossiper)   chusme'ar (to gossip)

embro'mar (to fool someone)

es'cabio (alcohol, spirits)

fan'gote (a lot of money)

fa'yuto/a (a fake, someone who says one thing and does another)

fi'aca (laziness)

fi'ambre (corpse)

'gamba (leg)

'ganga or **bi'coca** (bargain)

garrón (problem, difficulty)

gaso'lero (someone with a low budget to do things)

'gato (1. Prostitute 2. Car cricket)

gau'chada (favor)

gil/a (moron, dumb)

'grasa (tacky)

grata'rola (free, without any cost)

guaran'gada (insult, offensive gesture or saying)

¡gu'arda! (careful! - interjection)

'guita (money)

'joda (1.joke 2.problem or inconvenience)

jo'dido / jo'dida (difficult or mean person)

jo'vato/a (despective term for an old man or woman)

ju'nar (1.to see 2. to see through, guess intentions)

ki'lombo (mess)

labu'rar (to work)   **la'buro** (job, work)

las'trar (to eat)

la vi'eja (old lady: mother) **el vi'ejo** (old man: father) Also, **los vi'ejos** (parents)

ma'cana (1. inconvenience, problem 2. lie) **¡Qué ma'cana!** (What a problem!)

maca'nudo/a (cool, fine)

mama'rracho (a person who doesn't match or dresses badly)

'mango (peso, the Argentine currency) **mangue'ar** or **ti'rar la 'manga** (to ask something for free)

metejón (infatuation)

'mina (girl, woman)   minón (gorgeous, curvy woman)

mor'far (to eat) **'morfi** (food)

'mufa (1. someone who brings bad luck 2. anger)

'negro/a : a term used to call a close friend, similar to the English "darling" or "honey" (for a woman), and "dude" or "boy" (for a man). Literally : "black'.

'ojo or **o'jito** (interjection : careful! , watch out!)

o'tario (creep)

'palo (1. a million; 2. a road accident)

pa'vada (nonsense)

pe'tiso / a (short person)

pian'tado/a or **pi'rado/a** (nuts, crazy)
pi'rarse or **pian'tarse** (1. to become insane; 2. to leave in a hurry)

'piba (young girl) **'pibe** (young guy)

'pilcha (clothes)

pi'ola (streetwise)

pi'ropo (compliment, especially the non-agressive phrases that men say to a woman in the street. If it is vulgar, it is a "guarangada" not a "piropo".)

'plata (money)

'posta (reliable, true)

'pucho or **'faso** (cigarette)

quía (guy)

qui'lombo (problem, scandal, mess)

'ra'jar (1. to leave in a hurry. 2. to fire from work or dismiss from school)

rata (poor or broke)

ro'ñoso/a (dirty)

'sota (someone who being guilty pretends that nothing happened)

'tacho (taxicab) **ta'chero** (cab driver)

'tarro (good luck)

'timba (gambling) **timbe'ar** (to gamble) **tim'bero** (gambler)

'tipo /a (guy / woman)

tra'moya (trick, rip-off)

'trucho/a (1. fake. 2. something of the lowest quality)

'yapa (baker's dozen)

'yeta (bad luck)

za'pato (dummy, idiot)

(B) Sometimes the order of the syllables change and the word is read backwards. This use is less frequent now. Some examples of words still heard, here and there, are :

'broli : 'libro (book)

'feca : café (coffee, coffee-shop)

gar'par : pa'gar (to pay)

gomía : a'migo (friend)

gotán : 'tango

'jermu : mu'jer (woman, wife)

no'erma : her'mano (brother)

'novi : 'vino (wine)

¿Qué 'sapa? : ¿Qué pasa? (What's the matter?)

or'tiba : bati'dor (squealer)

ri'oba : barrio (neighborhood)

'rope : 'perro (dog)

'saca : 'casa (house)

'tordo : doc'tor

tro'esma : ma'estro (someone intelligent and respected)

'trompa : patrón (boss)

'zapie : pi'eza (room, bedroom)

'zapi : 'pizza

3. BU'ENOS MO'DALES
(Good Manners)

Basic phrases to learn :

Por fa'vor (please)

'Gracias (thanks)

'Muchas 'gracias (Thank you very much)

Perdón (Excuse me / Sorry)

'Hola (Hello / Hi)
¿Cómo está ? (How are you? - formal usted)

¿Qué tal? (What's up? - neutral)

¿Cómo andás? (What's up? - very informal vos)

- **Muy bi'en** (Very well, good, fine)

- **Geni'al / bárbaro / re-bi'en** (super, terrific, awesome)

- **Bien** (Well / fine)

- **Más o 'menos** (more or less, it depends)

- **Regu'lar** / qué sé yo (so so)

- **No muy bi'en** (not very well)

- **Re-'mal** (very badly)

Bu'enos días / Bu'en día (Good morning)

Bu'enas 'tardes (Good afternoon)

Bu'enas 'noches (Good evening / good night)

¿'Habla inglés? (Do you speak English? - formal = usted)

¿Hablás inglés? (Do you speak English? - informal = vos)

4. EN EL AEROPU'ERTO
(At the airport)

Phrases and vocabulary for your **lle'gada**
(arrival) and **sa'lida** (departure).

Acá ti'ene
...mi pasa'porte (Here's ...my passport)
...los pa'sajes (...the tickets)
...el formu'lario (...the form)

'Este es mi equi'paje (This is my baggage)

'Esas va'lijas son mías (Those suitcases are mine)

Nece'sito ...un ca'rrito (I need ...a cart / trolley)
...un male'tero (...a porter)
...un 'taxi (...a cab / taxi)
...trans'porte 'hasta mi ho'tel
  (...transportation to my hotel)
...cambi'ar 'plata (...to change money)
...ha'blar por teléfono (...to make a
  phonecall)

No 'tengo 'nada 'para decla'rar (I have
nothing to declare)

'Tengo 'esto 'para de'clarar (I have this to
declare)

¿'Tengo que a'brir ...el 'bolso? (Do I have
  to open ...the bag?)
...la va'lija? (...the suitcase?)

PORTEÑOS TALK

> ## What you can hear :

Pasa'porte... (Your passport, please)

¿Me permite su ...pasaporte? (Can I see
your passport?)
...pasaje? (... your ticket?)

'Abrame 'esta valija, por favor. (Open
this suitcase, please.)

5. EN EL HO'TEL
(At the hotel)

'Tengo una re'serva a 'nombre de ... (I have a reservation under ...-your name)

Nece'sito una habitación...single (I need a single room)
... 'doble (...double room)
... con 'cama matrimoni'al (...with a double bed)
... con bu'ena 'vista, por fa'vor (...with a nice view, please)

¿Ti'ene ...'aire acondicio'nado? (Does it have ...air conditioning?)
...calefacción? (...heating?)
...televisión? (...television?)
...'baño pri'vado? (...private bathroom? = en suite)

¿El ho'tel ti'ene 'caja de seguri'dad? (Is there a safety box in the hotel?)

¿A qué 'hora pu'edo reti'rar di'nero de la 'caja de seguri'dad? (What time can I withdraw money from the safety box?)

¿Cuál es el 'precio por 'noche? (What's the cost per night?)

¿In'cluye el desa'yuno? (Is breakfast included?)
Me voy a ...que'dar 'hasta el sábado. (I'm going to...stay until Saturday)
Nos 'vamos a ... (We're going to...)
Nece'sito ...to'allas (I need ...towels)
...fra'zadas (...blankets)
...una almo'hada (... a pillow)

...pa'pel higiénico (...toilet paper)
...jabón (...soap)
...que me despi'erten (...to be woken up)
...ser'vicio de lavandería (...some laundry done)
...información turística (...tourist information)
...un 'mapa (...a map)

Quisi'era desayu'nar en la habitación. (I'd like to have breakfast in my room.)

¿Me pre'para la cu'enta de la habitación 123? (Can I have the bill for room 123 ready?)

¿A qué 'hora hay que de'jar la habitación? (What time do I have to check out? ...I have to leave the room?)

> ### What you can hear :

¿Ti'ene re'serva? (Do you have a reservation?)
No hay más lu'gar. (There are no vacancies.)
Está com'pleto. (same)
No te'nemos habitaci'ones 'libres (There are no rooms available)
¿Pu'ede lle'nar la 'ficha? (Could you fill out this form?)

6. CAMBI'ANDO 'PLATA
(Changing money)

Most hotels will change money for you, usually at the **recepción** (reception). However you might find a better rate at a **'banco** (bank) or **'casa de 'cambio** (exchange bureau).
¿Dónde pu'edo cambi'ar 'plata? (Where can I change money?)

Nece'sito cambi'ar ...dólares, 'libras, 'marcos, 'liras, etc.. (I need to change Dollars, Pounds, Marks, Liras, etc.)
...'cheques de via'jero (traveller's checks)
...reti'rar di'nero con la tar'jeta (to withdraw money from my credit card)

¿Cuál es el 'cambio? (What's the exchange rate?)

¿'Cobran comisión? (Is there a charge?)

¿Me pu'ede dar ...bi'lletes de di'ez 'pesos? (Can I have $10 notes?)
... mo'nedas? (.... coins?)

What you can hear :

¿Me per'mite un docu'mento? (Can I see your ID?)
¿Qui'ere 'cambio? (Do you prefer small denominations?)

7. EN EL CO'RREO
(At the post office)

When you enter the **co'rreo** (post office) look for signs above the counters: **'simples** (regular letters and postcards), **certifi'cadas** (registered), **tele'gramas** (telegrams) or **multiser'vicio** (for all kinds). Don't worry about clarifying that you want to send them **vía aérea** (air mail). The clerks will assume that.

'Hola, ...'simple(s) por fa'vor. (Hello, ...re gular letters, please)
...certifi'cadas... (...registered...)
...'esta(s) 'simple(s) y 'esta certifi'cada... (...This/these is/are regular and this is registered...)

Qui'ero man'dar ...un tele'grama (I want to send ...a telegram)
...un pa'quete (...a packet)
...im'presos (...printed matter)
...un fax (... a fax)

Qui'ero com'prar estam'pillas (I want to buy stamps)

¿Dónde está la venta'nilla de 'poste res'tante? (Where's the General Delivery counter?)
¿Hay al'guna 'carta 'para...? (Are there any letters for...? - your name)

8. HA'BLANDO POR TELEFONO
(Making a phonecall)

Certainly you will be able to make a phonecall from the hotel, however it is more advisable to look for a **locu'torio** (public phone cabins/ booths), where charges will be less expensive, as they have "call back" services and discounts. Ask in the street, there are many around town.

¿Cuánto cu'esta el mi'nuto a...?
(What's the rate per minute to...? -your country)

¿A qué 'hora es más ba'rato? (What time is the reduced rate?)

¿Cuál es el pre'fijo de...? (what's the area code for...? -your country or city)

¿Es con dis'cado di'recto? (Is it direct dialing?)

Nece'sito a'yuda con la lla'mada. (I need help with this call.)

> What you can hear :

At the locutorio

¿Vá a ha'blar? (Are you going to make a phonecall?)
Pasé a la ca'bina 2 (You can use booth number 2.)

9. DE PA'SEO POR LA CIU'DAD
(Sightseeing)

¿Vos sos el / la guía de la excursión? (Are you the tour guide? - M/F - informal)

¿Us'ted es el cho'fer del 'micro? (Are you the bus/coach driver? - formal)

¿Adónde 'vamos ...hoy? (Where are we going ...today?)
... pri'mero? (... first?)

¿Por qué no 'vamos a 'Parque Le'zama? (Why don't we go to Parque Lezama?)

¿No po'demos ir a La 'Boca? (Can't we go to La Boca?)

¿Qué es ...ese edi'ficio? (What's ...that building?)
...esa es'tatua? (...that statue?)
...ese monu'mento? (...that monument?)

¿Cómo se 'llama ...'esa 'calle? (What's the name of ...that street?)
...'esta 'plaza? (...this square?)
... 'este 'barrio? (..this neighborhood?)

Me gustaría ir al Mu'seo de 'Bellas 'Artes. (I'd like to go to the Fine Arts Museum.)

Nos gustaría ver la Universi'dad de Bu'enos 'Aires (We'd like to see the University of B.A.)

¿Hay que pa'gar en'trada? (Is there a cover /an admission charge to pay?)

¿Se pu'eden sa'car 'fotos? (Is is possible to take pictures?)

Perdón, ¿nos podría sa'car una 'foto? (Excuse me, could you take a picture of us?)

¿Se pu'ede fil'mar? (Is it possible to videotape/ film?)

Me olvidé ...la cámara en el 'micro (I left ...my camera on the bus)
... la bille'tera en el ho'tel (... my wallet in the hotel)

¿A qué 'hora ...nos 'pasa a bus'car el 'micro? (What time does the bus/coach come to pick us up?)
...nos 'vamos 'para la Reco'leta? (...do we go to Recoleta?)
...nos 'vamos? (...do we leave?)

¿'Queda 'lejos El 'Tigre? (Is El Tigre far from here?)

What you can hear :

'Este/a es ... (This is...)
A la de'recha está... (To the right is...)
A la izqui'erda está... (To the left is ...)

Ade'lante está... (In front of us is...)

'Suban al 'micro. (Get on the bus)

A las 5 ...vol'vemos al 'micro. (At 5 we come back to the bus.)

... nos encon'tramos acá. (... we meet here.)

Nos 'vamos a que'dar 'hasta las 3. (We are going to stay here until 3.)

Acá hay que pa'gar en'trada. (We have to pay an admission ticket here.)

¿Quiéren que les 'saque 'una 'foto? (Do you want me to take a picture of you?)

10. DE 'COMPRAS
(Shopping)

-See also the numbers and colors appendix-

Perdón, ¿cuánto ...cu'esta 'esto? (Excuse me, how much does this cost?)
...'sale 'esto? (How much is this? - more informal)

'Hola, es'toy bus'cando un 'mate (Hello, I'm looking for a "mate".)

Es'toy mi'rando sola'mente (I'm just looking)

Es'taba mi'rando las re'meras (I am looking at the t-shirts.)

¿Us'ted es vende'dor / vende'dora? (Are you an assistant? -masculine/feminine- formal)

¿Vos sos ...? (Are you..? -informal)

¿Ti'ene Mastercard / Visa, etc.? (Do you take...?)

¿Ti'ene re'cargo con tar'jeta? (Is there an extra charge for credit cards?- a vital question)
¿Ti'ene descu'ento en efec'tivo? (Is there a discount for paying cash?)
¿Ti'ene lla'veros / posters/ souvenirs? (Do you have keyrings/ posters/souvenirs?)

¿Ti'ene 'algo ...más 'grande? (Do you have anything ...bigger/ larger?)

... me'jor? (... better?)

... más 'chico? (...smaller?)

... más ba'rato? (...cheaper/ less expensive?)

...de 'otro co'lor? (...in another color?)

Me pa'rece un 'poco 'caro. (I think it is a little expensive.)

Lo voy a pen'sar. (I'm going to think about it.)

Lo voy a lle'var. (I'll take it.)

No lo voy a lle'var a'hora. (I'm not going to buy it right now.)

No qui'ero 'nada a'hora, 'gracias. (I don't want anything now, thanks.)

> What you can hear :

Sí, bu'en día... (Yes, good morning - clerk addressing customer)

¿Lo ati'enden? ¿Lo atendi'eron? (Are you being attended? - formal)

¿Te ati'enden? ¿Te atendi'eron? (same, informal version "vos")

¿Qué an'daba bus'cando? (Are you looking for anything in particular? -formal "usted")

¿Qué an'dabas bus'cando? (informal "vos")

'Venga por acá. (Come this way.)

Te'nemos   'estas/os. (We have these.)

Son 'quince 'pesos. (It's fifteen pesos.)
¿En efec'tivo o con tar'jeta? (cash or charge?)
¿Un sólo 'pago? (one installment?)

Las o'fertas son en efec'tivo. (Sale items are to be paid cash.)
Las o'fertas no ti'enen descu'ento. (There are no discount on sale items.)

11. LOS 'MEDIOS DE TRANS'PORTE: TREN, SUBTE, COLECTIVO, TAXI Y REMIS
(Means of transport: train, subway, bus, taxi, and private cabs)

You can get around by a number of means in Buenos Aires. Get a city map, a subway map, or buy an inexpensive guide in the street, such as "Lumen" or "T" (for about 5 pesos) where you have everything, from detailed sections of all the neighborhoods to train routes and telephone numbers. Porteños have one of these guides in almost every home. Considering the dimensions of the city, it can be very handy.

If your idea is to stay in the **micro'centro** area, you might as well consider seeing Buenos Aires on foot - if the weather permits. Otherwise, think about the subway.

TREN :

¿Dónde están las venta'nillas? (Where are the ticket counters?)

'Uno, 'ida a 'Tigre. (One ticket, one way to Tigre.)

Tres, 'ida y vu'elta a San Fer'nando. (Three, round-trip to San Fernando.)

¿Cuánto es? (How much is it?)

¿A qué 'hora 'sale el próximo a Mar del 'Plata?
(When does the next train to Mar del Plata leave?)

'Clase tu'rista (economy class for long distance traveling)

'Clase pullman (business class)

Pri'mera 'clase (first class)

¿De qué andén 'sale el tren 'para Adrogué? (Which platform does the train to Adrogue leave from?)

el gu'arda (the inspector)

el perso'nal de seguri'dad (security guards)

What you can hear :

Bo'letos... (Tickets, please.)

'SUBTE :

Subways use **cos'peles** (tokens) that you have to purchase at one of the counters in every station. Each token is a single fare, which allows you to travel anywhere until the moment you exit the station.

'Uno, por fa'vor. (One please)

¿'Este va para Pa'lermo? (Does this one go

to Palermo?)

¿'Para la estación Tribu'nales, es 'este? (Is this the one to Tribunales station?)

¿'Para ha'cer combinación con la línea B, dónde 'tengo que ba'jar?
(Where do I have to get off to make a connection with line B?)

¿Por dónde es la combinación con la C?
(How do I connect with line C?)

> What you can hear or say :

Per'miso. (Excuse me. - Asking people to let you pass to get off or move)

¿'Baja? (Are you getting off? - usted)

¿Bajás? (Are you getting off? - vos)

COLEC'TIVO :

To pay the fare you will need coins; notes are not accepted.

'Hasta la ave'nida Corri'entes, ¿cuánto es?
(How much is it to Corrientes avenue?)

¿'Llega 'hasta Riva'davia al 2700? (Do you go as far as 2700 Rivadavia?)

¿Me 'deja 'cerca del zoológico? (Do you go near the zoo?)

¿'Falta 'mucho 'para lle'gar a Re'tiro? (Is it far to Retiro?)

Pa'rada por 'favor. (Stop please - if you cannot reach the back door/bell on time)

What you can hear :

¿'Hasta dónde vá? (Where are you going to/ getting off?)

¿'Baja en 'esta? (Do you want to get off at the next stop?)

TAXI :

Taxis have fare counters in pesos, and are relatively affordable. You can expect to pay between $2 to $4 for a twenty block drive, depending on traffic lights. There is also a starting amount (about $1) for the trip, so do not be surprised if you see the counter is not at zero.
Be careful with your personal belongings.

Bu'en día. 'Hasta 'Santa Fé y Ca'llao. (Good morning. To Santa Fé and Callao.)

Voy a 'Plaza San Martín. (I'm going to Plaza San Martín.)
'Vamos a... (We are going to...)

¿Cuánto es? (How much is it? - even though you can see the counter in pesos.)

Por acá está bien. (I can get out here.)

What you can hear :

¿'Hasta dónde vá? (Where to?)

¿Por dónde prefi'ere ir? (Which way would you like to go?)

¿En la es'quina? (Is it allright at the corner?)

¿Cru'zando o 'antes de cru'zar? (This corner or across the street?)

REMIS

Private cabs have become very popular lately, and many middle class people use them. They are convenient, sometimes cheaper than a taxi, and reliable, as you call an agency to ask for a car.
You can see many agencies : **a'gencia de remís, re'misses** or similar spellings, around town, or look for one in the **páginas**

ama'rillas (yellow pages) or **guía telefónica** (phone book). You have to call them and tell them where you want to go, your address, and telephone number. And you can ask how much the fare is in advance. They pick you up at your home or hotel.

'Tengo que ir 'hasta Bel'grano, a la 'calle Solís. (I have to go to Belgrano - a neighborhood -, to Solís street.)
Mi dirección es... (My address is...)

Mi teléfono es... (My telephone is...)

¿Cuánto 'sale el vi'aje? (How will the trip be?)

¿Vi'ene ense'guida? (Will it come straight away?)

¿Cuánto de'mora? (How long is the wait? - for the cab to get to your place)

Lo es'pero en la pu'erta (I'll be waiting at the door.)

What you can hear :

Besides the phrases listed in "Taxi" :

¿Pidió un remís? (Did you call for a remís?)

12. 'HORA DE CO'MER
(Time to eat)

¿Me pu'ede tra'er ...una 'carta/ un menú por fa'vor? (Could you bring ...the menu, please?)
...la cu'enta? (... the check/ bill?)

¿Nos pu'ede co'brar por sepa'rado, por fa'vor? (Can you charge us separately, please?)

> ### What you can hear :

Ya le 'traigo la 'carta. (I'll bring you the menu right away.)
¿Qui'ere 'algo más? (Do you want anything else?)
¿Le 'traigo 'algo más? (Can I bring you anything else?)

En se'guida. (Right away!)
Cómo no. (Sure!)
Ya se lo 'traigo. (I'll bring it right away.)
Acá ti'ene. (Here you are.)

¿Está 'todo en órden? (Is everything allright?)
¿Café? ¿'Postre? (Coffee? Any desserts?)

DESA'YUNO Y MERI'ENDA (breakfast and tea)

Qui'ero ...un café con 'leche, con media'lunas. (I'd like ...caffe late/coffee and milk, with croissants)
...un 'jugo de na'ranja. (... an orange juice)

...tos'tadas con man'teca y merme'lada.
(...toast with butter and jam)
...un cor'tado 'chico. (...small coffee
with a drop of milk)
...un té con limón. (... tea with lemon.)
...dos cafés. (...two small coffees)
...hu'evos revu'eltos (...scrambled eggs)
... 'leche y cere'al (...milk and cereal)
...yo'gurt (...yoghurt)

ALMU'ERZO Y 'CENA (lunch and supper)

¿Qué 'trae ...el menú ejecu'tivo? (What's
on the a la carte menu?)
...el 'pollo a la Car'litos? (...chicken a la
Carlitos?)

¿Qué es un tos'tado 'mixto? (What is a
"tostado mixto"? - a toasted, very thin ham
and cheese sandwich.)

Un super'pancho. (A jumbo hot dog)

Un choripán (A sausage sandwich)

Un 'triple de jamón y to'mate. (A thin
triple ham and tomato sandwich)

Un pe'bete de sa'lame. (A salami sandwich in
a bun.)

**Una porción de 'tarta de ver'dura / ce'bolla
/ jamón y 'queso , etc.** (A slice of pie :
spinach / onion / ham and cheese.

Dos empa'nadas de 'carne / de jamón y 'queso / de 'pollo / de hu'mita , etc. (Two "empanadas" -patties /pasties- made of beef / ham and cheese/ chicken/ corn paste, etc..)

Una 'grande de muzza'rella (A large mozzarella cheese pizza)

Una porción de muzza'rella y otra napoli'tana.
(A slice of cheese pizza and another "napolitana" - fresh tomatoes, garlic, and cheese.)

Un 'bife con 'papas 'fritas y ensa'lada 'mixta.
(A steak with french fries and with a lettuce and tomato salad.)

Una hambur'guesa com'pleta. (A burguer - usually with : lettuce, tomatoes, onion, and cheese)

Una mila'nesa con puré. (A breaded fried thin steak with mashed potatoes.)

Vacío al 'horno con 'papas (Roast beef and potatoes)

Ravi'oles con 'tuco. (Ravioli and tomato sauce.)

A'rroz con 'pollo. (Rice and chicken)
Parri'llada. (barbecued cow's offal)

A'sado de 'tira. (beef with bones)

Ma'tambre con 'rusa. (beef roll stuffed with carrots, eggs, peppers, etc., with a Russian salad : potatoes, carrots, green beans and mayonaise)

'Bife de cho'rizo. (filet mignon)

Pas'tel de 'papas. (shepherd's pie)

BE'BIDAS (drinks)

'Agua mine'ral con gas (gasified mineral water)
'Agua mine'ral sin gas. (still mineral water)

'Tinto de la 'casa (house red : red wine, without any preferences)

'Blanco de la 'casa (house white : any white wine)

'Soda (gasified plain water)

Una 'coca / sprite, etc (a coke, etc.).

Cer'veza (beer)

Bo'tella de tres cu'artos (a ¾ liter bottle : for beer or wine)

'POSTRES (Desserts)

He'lado de fru'tilla y choco'late / vai'nilla
(ice cream, chocolate and strawberry,
vanilla)

Ensa'lada de 'frutas (fruit salad)

Flan con 'dulce de 'leche / con 'crema. (flan
with fudge or "milk jam" / with whipped
cream.)

Una 'tarta de man'zana. (a slice of apple
pie)

13. ENTRETENIMI'ENTO
(Entertainment)

If you stop by a tourist office in the downtown you can get a free copy of the BS AS Guide, with a listing of restaurants, plays, concerts, bars, clubs, etc.

¿Podés recomen'darme 'algo? (Can you recommend anything? - vos)

¿Pu'ede recomen'darme ...'algo? (Can you recommend anything? - usted)
    ...una película? (...a movie?)
    ...una 'obra de te'atro? (...a play?)
    ... un bar? (...a bar?)
    ...un lu'gar 'para ir a bai'lar? (a place to go dancing?)
    ...un lu'gar 'para co'mer? (a place to eat?)

¿A qué 'hora empi'eza? (What time does it start?)

¿Cuánto cu'esta la en'trada? (How much is the cover / admission ticket?)

¿Cómo hay que ir ves'tido? (What should I wear?)

¿Es un lu'gar ...for'mal? (Is it a formal place?)
    ...infor'mal? (...an informal place?)

¿Es 'caro? (Is it expensive?)
¿Dónde están los 'baños? (Where are the restrooms?)

What you can hear or say :

Invitations :

¿Querés bai'lar? (Do you want to dance?)

¿Bailás? (Want to dance?)

¿Querés to'mar 'algo? (Do you want something to drink?)

¿Querés ir ...a co'mer? (Would you like to go ...eat something?)
   ...al 'cine? (...to the movies?)

Bu'eno ['gracias] (Ok [thanks])
No ['gracias] (No [thanks])

Me encantaría. (I'd love to).

No me inte'resa. (I'm not interested.)

14. EL LENGU'AJE DE LOS JOVENES
(The language of young people)

All words in the Lunfardo section (A) plus the ones here.

Reference :

[T] : teens and early twenties
[20] : late twenties
[A] : all
[R] :rude

The preffix "re" (very / really) used to give emphasis is widely used in young people's speech, and sometimes by adults. Nonetheless, teenagers are perhaps the ones who have adopted it the most - in almost every sentence they say.

Favorable opinions :

Es re-'lindo/'linda - Está re-bu'eno/bu'ena (it's very nice) [A], mostly [T]

Ti'ene 'onda (it's cool)[A] - **Está co'pado/ co'pada** [T]

Me 'cabe (I like it)[T]

Negative opinions :

Es re-difícil (it's very difficult)
Es re-ta'rado/a (He/she is a super moron)

Es de cu'arta/ Es de última (it stinks)[A]

No me 'cabe. (I don't like it)[T]

No me lo 'banco. (I don't like it) [A]

Es una mi'erda/ca'gada (it's shit/crap)[R]

Basic glossary   (words and phrases):

a'greta (bitter person) Mostly [20]

al 'mango (at full speed, energetic, high volume) [A]

al 'toque (fast or right away) [20]

bajón (down / low period) [A]

bajone'ar (to depress/ be depressed) e.g. **Me bajo'nea la política.** (Politics depress me) [A]

ban'car (1.to tolerate. 2.to stand by someone) [A]

barde'ar (to cause problems or make fuss) [A]

'bardo (problem, mess, something negative) [A]

bo'liche (bar, dance club) [A]

bo'ludo/bo'luda (used as an appellative, rather than an insult; usually preceded by "che") e.g. **Che, bo'luda, 'vamos.** (Hey girl, let's go) [T] [R]

bo'rrarse (1. To leave in a hurry or disappear as in **"Me borré"** : I left. / 2. To forget as in **"Se me borró"** : I forgot that) [A]

bu'ena 'onda (adjective : nice, kind)
'mala 'onda (negative, boring)
Te'ner bu'ena 'onda (to be positive, optimistic)
Te'ner 'mala 'onda (to be pesimistic) [A]

ca'reta (1. rich people 2. those who frown upon drugs) [A]

carete'ar (to behave like rich people, yuppies, etc.) [A]

col'gar (to deceive or disappoint somebody) e.g. **Me colgó.** (He/She let me down) [A]

col'gado/col'gada (1. very inadequate or out of place as in **"Es un col'gado"** : He is so inadequate [A] / 2. Someone without a girlfriend or boyfriend as in **"Estoy re-colgado"** : I don't have anyone to go out with. [T])

¿cómo? (interjection : Sure!) [T]

'corki (stupid) [T]

¡Cor'tala! (Quit it!, Pack it in!) [A]

cor'tar el 'rostro (to reject or turn someone down)

¿Cuál es? (I don't care, whatever) [A]

cúbico/cúbica (stubborn) e.g. **'Esa 'mina es re-cúbica.** (That girl is so stubborn) [T]
cur'tir (1. to make out 2. to have sex) [A]

chabón (dude) [A]

cha'pita (nuts, crazy) Mostly [20]

'dado vu'elta (tripping after the effect of drugs/alcohol) e.g. **Está 'dado vu'elta.** (He is tripping out) [A]

'dale (interjection : Yes, fine) [A]

dar 'bola or **dar pe'lota** (to pay attention, be interested) [A] **no dar 'bola/ pe'lota** (to ignore)
de la ca'beza (crazy, nuts) [A] e.g. **Está de la cabeza.** (He/she is nuts.)

'denso (a drag, someone who is a pain in the butt) [A]

e'char flí (turn down, reject) [A]

em'bole (boredom as in **"Qué em'bole"** : How boring! Or I'm very bored!) [A]

fi'era (someone smart and cool) Mostly [20]

fisu'rado (exhausted or with a hangover) [A]

'flaco/'flaca (dude/girl) [20]

flashe'ar (to become amazed or find something deep) e.g. **Me flasheó la película.** (The movie was amazing/deep) [T]

fra'nela (kisses and caresses)
franele'ar (to kiss and caress) [A]

garrón (bummer) [A]

ha'cer la 'gamba or **ha'cer el agu'ante** (to stand by someone) [A]

¡'joya! (cool! - interjection) [A]
'mambo (craziness) e.g. Ti'ene un 'mambo... (He/She is so crazy) [A]

'masa (very cool) [T]

mi'nita (girl) [A]

'nabo (geek or moron) [A]

¡'obvio! / ¡'obvia'mente! (sure! - interjection) [A]

'onda (vibe) As in **bu'ena 'onda** or **'mala 'onda** (good or bad vibes, used also as adjectives). **Ten'er 'onda** (to be cool) and **de 'onda** (good intentions). [A]

pálida (bad news, negative opinion, bad

mood) Mostly [20]

pal'mar (1. to die; 2. to be exhausted as in "Palmé" : I'm beaten) [A]

po'nerse las 'pilas (to get the hang of it / concentrate or get going) e.g. **'Tengo que po'nerme las 'pilas 'para el e'xamen** (I have to concentrate and study for the exam) [A]
'potro / a (beautiful guy or girl) [A]

rebo'tar (to turn down, reject) [A]

sa'car (to infuriate) [20]
sa'cado/ a (crazy, nuts) [20]

¡'Todo bi'en! / ¡'Todo 'joya! / ¡'Todo o'key! (Everything's cool!) [A]

'traga (nerd) [A]

'transa (one night stand, fast love) [A]
tran'sar (to have sex) [T]

'trolo (gay) [A]   **'trola** (1. lesbian 2. easy girl) [T]

un 'toco, 'un pe'dazo or **'una 'pila** (a great deal, a lot) [A]

un 'pomo or **'una 'goma** (nothing) [A]

vi'eja (dude) e.g. **¿'Para dónde vas vi'eja?** (Where are you going, dude?) [T]

15. 'MALAS PA'LABRAS E IN'SULTOS
(Swearing and cursing)

Let me first warn you that these words and phrases can be very dangerous to use, and can get you in trouble. However, they are part of our vocabulary. Since many people use them -with various kinds of effects- it seems likely that you will come across one, and in that event I think you should know exactly what is meant.

Effects vary according to the speaker's tone of voice, which indicates whether he/she is joking, uses it in a mild way or not. Many porteños use curses in a harmless way, as in "Che, boludo", (a phrase to call a friend). No offence is implied by that.

Qualifying, offering negative and positive opinions :

... **de mi'erda** (shitty) a negative adjective; e.g. **una película de mi'erda.**

... **de la 'puta 'madre** (mother fucking) a positive adjective; e.g. **una fi'esta de la 'puta 'madre** : a mother fucking party.

Expressing annoyance or surprise : (the effect varies with the tone of voice)

¡La 'puta!
¡La mi'erda!
¡Que lo parió!

¡Qué ca'gada!

¡La 'puta 'madre!

¡La 'puta que lo parió!

¡La re-'puta 'madre!

What someone can be called :

Bo'ludo /a or **pelo'tudo/a** (asshole; almost literally "big balls")

Gu'acho / gu'acha (bastard)

'Hijo de 'puta /'hija... (son of a bitch)

Cagón /ca'gona (chicken shit)

'Forro/a (prick; literally "condom")

Hinchape'lotas or 'rompe-pe'lotas (ball breaker)

Pen'dejo/ a (brat, someone childish or immature)

Idioms :

Ca'gar a 'palos or **ca'gar a pa'tadas** (to reprimand verbally or physically)

Ca'garse de 'risa (to crack up/ laugh hard)

Ce'rrar el 'culo / el 'orto (to shut up)

Es'tar al 'pedo (to do nothing or have nothing to do)

Es'tar en 'pedo (to be drunk or out of one's mind)

Ha'cer bolu'deces (to act in a stupid way)

Hacerse el boludo/ el pelotudo/ el otario, etc. (to play dumb, pretend nothing happened)

Ha'cer las 'cosas 'para el ca'rajo / 'para la mi'erda (to do things badly)

'Irse al ca'rajo (1.to leave suddenly 2. to come up with something ridiculous)

Me'ar fu'era del 'tarro (to do something the wrong way -- literally "to pee outside the jar")

No ha'cer un ca'rajo/ una mi'erda (to do nothing at all)

Rom'per las pe'lotas (to bust somebody's balls)

Ser 'culo inqui'eto (to be hyperactive)

Ser 'culo y calzón (to be very close friends with somebody)

Te'ner hor'migas en el 'culo (to be hyperactive -- literally "to have ants in one's butt")

Te'ner las 'bolas 'llenas / por el 'piso (to be tired about a situation or a person)

Te'ner 'culo (to be lucky)

Ti'rar a la mi'erda / al ca'rajo (to throw something away)

16. 'PARA NO PER'DERSE
(Don't miss it)

Getting to know a new place involves not only visiting museums or tourist attractions. For some travelers a special delight can be found in the exploration of an unknown territory, and the culture of its inhabitants. After all, isn't it really the people who make a place what it is?
This section is about our lifestyle. I'll try to show you the backbone of our culture to the best of my knowledge.

Whenever I travel abroad I carry a **'mate** (gourd) with me, with a **bom'billa** (metal straw with holes) and enough supply of **'yerba** or **'yerba 'mate** (a kind of tea) for my stay. **'Mate** drinking is a daily habit. Most of us have it for breakfast, in the afternoon, and of course on any occasion that calls for it : chatting with friends, sitting in the kitchen with grandma, etc. **Ce'bar 'mate** (the ceremony of pouring mate) is a ritual.

And on a final note, you have to know that the word *"mate"* is used for all three : the drink, the tea and the container. Try experimenting with a mate ready to have (*"Mate Listo"*) or in tea bags, that can be found at **qui'oscos** (the thousand mini stores you can see everywhere, like tiny drugstores) in the **Ciu'dad de Buenos Aires**, also called **la capi'tal.** You only need to add sugar, as it tends to have a bitter taste, and hot water (never boil it).

I'm sure you have also heard that Buenos

Aires has excellent beef to offer. Several **pa'rrilas** (steak houses) prove that. I would certainly recommend a simple **'bife con 'papas 'fritas** (steak with french fries) and if you like spicy food, ask for a dressing called **chimi'churri.** Don't leave Buenos Aires without trying the local **cer'veza** (beer) such as *'Quilmes.*

However when it comes to food, what I miss the most abroad is something called **'sanguches** or **sandwiches de 'miga**, very thin, white bread assorted sandwiches that you can find at the **panaderías** (baker's). Step into one and ask for : **'una do'cena de 'sanguches de 'miga, sur'tidos** (a dozen assorted sandwiches) or as a sample, only two or three sandwiches. You won't regret it. Traditionally we love to go to a **cumple'años** (birthday party) and eat them.

And while you are at the **panadería**, have a look at the **fac'turas** (pastries), like **media'lunas** (croissants), **'churros** (fried sticks), **vigi'lantes** (sticks with jam and creme brulee), **cañon'citos de 'dulce de 'leche** (rolls stuffed with milk jam) and others. All are excellent to have with mate for example. They are usually sold by the dozen (around $4) or half a dozen, but you can always buy less.

Speaking of **'dulce de 'leche** (milk jam), if you have a sweet tooth, you will love it in all its forms. Get a small **'pote** (jar) at an

almacén (grocery store) or **supermer'cado** (supermarket) -good brands are *"La Serenísima", "Gándara",* and *"Sancor"*- with a **pa'quete de galle'titas** (packet of crackers) like *"Criollitas"* or *"Express"*, and enjoy!

Another way to taste this jam is as the filling of an **alfa'jor,** a type of biscuit. You can buy one at any **qui'osco**. They really are a classic among schoolchildren, students or business people. Try any variety: **choco'late** or **'dulce de 'leche. Alfa'jores** are a delicacy also found in cities on the Atlantic shore, coming in several flavors. In Buenos Aires you can find these more refined versions at *"Havana"*, a store from Mar del Plata..

And finally, if you search the counter of your local **quios'quero** (kiosk's owner) you can find **'dulce de 'leche** in candy bars, sweeties, etc.

My last tip concerning edibles is **garrapi'ñadas de maní** or **de al'mendras** (peanuts or almonds with a sugary coat). You can see vendors at the corners, flipping them inside a copper pan on a precarious stove. They come in a plastic bag, for about $1.

When you are in the **micro'centro**, go people watching on Florida, specially near Plaza San Martín, where you will see all the

well-dressed, stylish business people.
However, if you want to get into the heart
of it, go to the financial district - an area
surrounded by streets (and smog, I'm afraid) :
Florida, Paseo Colón, Bartolomé Mitre and
Corrientes. Eat with all the **ofici'nistas**
(clerks, white collars) in the **cafeterías,**
'bares or **cafés** (coffee shops). Look for
signs in the windows, advertising combo
platters.

El **'barrio de San 'Telmo** (San Telmo
neighborhood) is also worth visiting. On
weekends, there are two **'ferias** (markets) :
for **antigüe'dades** (antiques) and street
performers at *Plaza Dorrego*, and **artesanías**
(crafts) at *Parque Lezama.*
Across from the **Facul'tad de De'recho** (Law
School), on *Libertador* and *Pueyrredón*,
there is a park called *"Plaza Francia"*, where
you can find another **'feria de artesanías**,
performers, bands, etc. on Saturdays and
Sundays. Try going to the **facul'tad** on a
weekday, and visit one of the schools that
belong to **Universi'dad de Buenos Aires**
across the avenue. It might be interesting to
have a look at hundreds of students along
the halls, in the cafeteria, etc.

That's also part of our daily routines, as it is
reading the **di'ario** (newspaper) such as
Clarín - the most popular one. On Fridays
there is a section for young people called
"Sí", with a concert calendar, as well as
the show guide in the *Espectáculos* section,

with a long listing of plays, movies, concerts, dance, etc. for the **fin de se'mana** (weekend). A fantastic and very complete leisure section comes with *La Nación* newspaper on Fridays, and it is called *"Vía Libre"*.

At the **qui'osco de di'arios y re'vistas** (newsstand - literally: newspapers and magazines stand), you will also find other papers *"Crónica"*, *"Página 12"*, etc. and publications like *"Segundamano"* - for second hand items -, local **re'vistas** specialized on show business, like *"Gente"* and *"Caras"*, etc. and *"The Buenos Aires Herald"*, a newspaper in English. Among the many comics, look for **Ma'falda** - a girl philosopher who is almost a national hero to several generations. Other good options are **Isi'doro** (a typical high class porteño), **Patoruzú** (a gaucho super hero), and **Matías** (a boy who asks and questions everything).

On weekends, many people like going for a walk in a park like those mentioned earlier. And also walking along Corrientes, from the **Obe'lisco** to Callao avenue, where you find many **librerías** (bookstores). People just step in and have a look around. There are **cafés** and **'cines** (cinemas), as well as theatres. Go inside the **"Teatro San Martín"** where most plays are very affordable! And while you are there, visit the free **Fotogalería** (photo gallery), which has interesting exhibitions.

Corrientes avenue is also popular for shopping for inexpensive clothes, shoes and accessories. While other neighborhoods, commercial centers or malls have a special appeal to wealthier folks or tourists, **El Once** (Once neighborhood) is the best kept secret for all of us who hate to pay excessively high prices. Take the **'subte** (subway), **línea B** (B line), towards Federico Lacroze terminal and get off at Pasteur or Pueyrredón stations. Both are half way through the heart of "El Once", which is Corrientes and Paso - bargain city!

Certainly not to miss here is a good **par'tido de fútbol** (soccer/ football match), especially a final. Much better when the teams are archrivals like "Boca Juniors" vs "River Plate" or "Racing" vs "Independiente". If you don't care much for crowds so as to go to **la 'cancha** (the stadium), watch it on TV at one of the bars where everybody gathers to **hin'char por los e'quipos** (root for the teams).

Cable TV is probably no different here than at home in your country. You can find CNN, ESPN, HBO, etc. However, tune into one of our five local **ca'nales** (channels) : "7" - owned by the state - or the private "Azul TV", "Telefé", "América" and "Canal 13". Some of the most popular **pro'gramas** (shows) - those that people talk about the following day - are **"Campeones"** and **"Videomatch".** Cult shows, at press time,

watched by young people are on after 11pm
such as **"Vulnerables"**, and **"El Rayo"**.
Check the newspaper for the hours.

Radio offers a good range of **estaci'ones**
(stations). "FM Tango" and "FM Clásica"
are devoted to **'tango** and classical music
respectively. "Rock and Pop FM" has a
young audience : Listen to "¿Cuál es?", at 9
AM on R&P, hosted by Mario Pergolini; and "
Animal de radio", at 7 PM, hosted by Lalo
Mir. At midnight, don't miss "La venganza
será terrible" on AM radio station
"Continental", hosted by Alejandro Dolina, a
classic for several years now. You can even
go see it live - usually at the "Café Tortoni"
(on De Mayo avenue and Esmeralda) from
Mon. to Thu.(it's best to check first).
Music to take back with you include the
following options :

For tango : Artists like Roberto Goyeneche,
Adriana Varela, Astor Piazzola, Julio Sosa or
Carlos Gardel.

Rock and pop with a local flavor : Charly
García, Luis Alberto Spinetta, Soda Stereo,
Divididos, Los Piojos, Las Pelotas, La
Portuaria and Man Ray, among many
bands.

17. 'VEINTE 'DICHOS POPU'LARES

(Twenty popular sayings)

Beside each proverb you will find an equivalent in English, which maybe not the literal translation, but the closest version.

-**A ca'ballo rega'lado no se le 'miran los di'entes.** (Don't look a gift horse in the mouth.)

-**A 'falta de pan, bu'enas son 'tortas.** (Half a loaf is better than no bread.)

-**Al que ma'druga, Dios lo a'yuda.** (The early bird catches the worm.)

-**'Aunque la 'mona se 'vista de 'seda, 'mona 'queda.** (You can't make a silk purse out of a sow's ear.)

-**Dónde 'hubo fu'ego, ce'nizas 'quedan.** (Where there's smoke, there's fire.)

-**El hábito no 'hace al 'monje.** (Don't judge a book by its cover.)

-**El que no 'llora no 'mama.** (The squeaky wheel gets the grease.)

-**El que ríe último, ríe me'jor.** (He who laughs last, laughs best.)

-**Es'coba nu'eva, 'barre bien.** (A new broom sweeps clean.)

-**Las 'malas no'ticias 'llegan rápido.** (Bad news travel fast.)

-**Los 'polos opu'estos se a'traen.** (Opposites atract.)

-**Más 'vale pájaro en 'mano que ci'en vo'lando.** (A bird in the hand is worth two in the bush.)

-**Más 'vale 'tarde que 'nunca.** (Better late than never.)

-**'Muchas 'manos en un 'plato 'hacen 'mucho gara'bato.** (Too many cooks spoil the broth.)

-**No 'dejes 'para ma'ñana lo que pu'edas ha'cer hoy.** (Never put off till tomorrow what you can do today.)

-**No hay que escu'pir 'para a'rriba.** (Don't spit into the wind.)

-**No 'todo lo que re'luce es 'oro.** (All that glitters is not gold.)

-**'Ojos que no ven, corazón que no si'ente.** (Out of sight, out of mind.)

-**'Perro que 'ladra, no mu'erde.** (A barking dog never bites.)

-**Una golon'drina no 'hace ve'rano.** (One swallow doesn't make a summer.)

18. APENDICE 1

URUGUAY : THE SPANISH HEARD IN MONTEVIDEO

If you visit Montevideo you will discover that the Spanish variety used there is surprinsingly similar to the language of Buenos Aires. As a matter of fact the inhabitants of that city are also called **Porteños** .

One of the most evident changes is the use of the pronoun "tú". In Uruguay it is common a mixed form, since people use *"tú"* with the verbs conjugated in "vos". For example : "Tú tenés" (you have). In Argentina this would be "Vos tenés"; while in Spain this becomes "Tú tienes".
On the other hand, some Uruguayans also employ the pronoun "vos" informally - even though there is a certain stigma as regards its lower status.

Slang words and phrases like : "boliche", "gil", or "franelear" are part of their daily vocabulary.
Curses, on the other hand are clearly understood, but not as common as in Buenos Aires, where they can also imply a degree of closeness and belonging (refer to chapter 15).

Other words heard in Uruguay are related to their own history and local costumes. For example, and even though tango is as popular there as it is in Buenos Aires, Uruguayans also have a deeply-rooted **"can'dombe"** tradition (a rhythm and dance of the African-Uruguayan community with a very contagious beat; also the name of a long drum). And therefore many common words derive from this, such as :

Carna'val : the equivalent of Mardi Grass, a popular celebration in Uruguay.
'Murga : a band of street musicians and actors, who do performances and parades especiallyat the "Carnaval" time.
Mur'guistas : the members of a "murga".
More'nada : a group of African-Uruguayan musicians, especially drum players.
'Negros : a common, friendly term for African-Uruguayans.

The following is a very basic glossary of terms used in Montevideo :

Apicho'narse : to become sick or to catch a cold.

Bichi'come : bum, homeless.

Biz'cochos : pastries ("facturas" in Buenos Aires)

Boti'ja : boy or girl, specially in the countryside area.

Buque, 'bondi, 'omnibus : bus

Calde'rita de 'lata : an impatient person.

Can'tar flor : to die, to break down as in "La radio cantó flor." (The radio is broken - and can't be repaired).

Cante'gril : precarious housing sector, shanty town.

Cara'vanas : small earrings

Crá : brilliant person, genious.

Champi'ones : sneakers.

'Chiva : bicycle.

Chi'vito : sirloin sandwich, very popular in Uruguay.

'Chongo/a : simple, low-quality.

Chu'minga : poor.

De la 'planta : awesome.

Do'blado : drunk.

Empi'jado : (vulgar) very busy, hectic.

En 'pila : (phrase) a lot .

Entre'vero : mess.

Frankfruter : frank, hot dog.

Gua'sadas : nonsense, vulgar expression.
Gurí : little boy or girl. (plural : guríses)

La quedé : (phrase) Bummer!, I screwed up!

Li'ceo : high school.

Ma'chete : scrooge, tight-fisted.

Marché : I screwed it!

'Medio y 'medio : drink made of wine and champagne.

Mere'cidas : (phrase) You're welcome.

Me'ter 'lomo : to work hard, make an effort.

Mongólico : dumb.

'Morras : man's legs.

Mejicane'ar : To fool a person (for example, stealing someone's girlfriend).

Mu'chacho/a : boy/ girl (not : "chico", "chica" as in Bs. As.)

Portugués : someone who constantly asks for and/or obtains things without paying for them.

Qué no, ni no : (phrase) Come on! Let's go!

Rela'jar : to insult, call names.

Rema'char : 1. to damage or hurt someone. 2. To kill someone.

Tá : (interjection) O.K., Fine!

Te'rraja : (vulgar) vulgar person or object.

Tor'tuga :   round sandwich, in a bun.

19. APENDICE 2

DIAS : (days)

'lunes (Monday)
'martes (Tuesday)
miércoles (Wednesday)
ju'eves (Thursday)
vi'ernes (Friday)
sábado (Saturday)
do'mingo (Sunday)

'MESES : (months)

e'nero (January)
fe'brero (February)
'marzo (March)
a'bril (April)
'mayo (May)
'junio (June)
'julio (July)
a'gosto (August)
septi'embre (September)
oc'tubre (October)
novi'embre (November)
dici'embre (December)

NUMEROS : (numbers)

0= 'cero
1= 'uno
2= dos
3= tres
4= cu'atro
5= 'cinco
6= seis

7= si'ete
8= 'ocho
9= nu'eve
10= di'ez
11= 'once
12= 'doce
13= 'trece

14= ca'torce
15= 'quince
16= di'eci'seis
17= di'ecisi'ete
18= di'eci'ocho
19= di'ecinu'eve
20= 'veinte

21= veinti'uno
22= veinti'dos, etc.
30= 'treinta
31= 'treinta y 'uno, etc
40= cua'renta
50= cincu'enta
60= se'senta
70= se'tenta
80= o'chenta
90= no'venta
100= ci'en
101= ci'ento 'uno, etc.
1000 = mil
2000= dos mil, etc.
10.000= di'ez mil
11.000= 'once mil
20.000= 'veinte mil, etc.
100.000= ci'en mil
1.000.000 = un millón
2.000.000= dos mi'llones, etc.

'HORA : (Time)

la una (1 o'clock)
las dos (2 o'clock.)
las tres (3 o'clock.)

las cu'atro (4 o'clock.)
las 'cinco (5 o'clock.)
las 'seis (6 o'clock.)
las si'ete (7 o'clock.)
las 'ocho (8 o'clock.)
las nu'eve (9 o'clock.)
las di'ez (10 o'clock.)
las 'once (11 o'clock.)
las 'doce (12 o'clock.)

Also to be more specific: **las si'ete de la ma'ñana** (7 AM, in the morning), etc. as well as **las tres de la 'tarde** (3 PM, afternoon), and **las 'ocho de la 'noche** (8 PM, in the evening).

The 24 hour system is also common. Therefore, after **las 'doce del mediodía** (twelve noon), 1 PM can be called **las 'trece** (13:00); 2PM becomes **las ca'torce** (14:00), and so on until **las veinticu'atro** (24:00) or **media'noche** (midnight).

MI'NUTOS (minutes) :

...y... (after / past) :
7:05 = **si'ete y 'cinco**
10:12 = **di'ez y 'doce**
1:15 = **una y 'quince** or **una y cu'arto**
4:20 = **cu'atro y 'veinte**
9:30= **nu'eve y 'treinta** or **nu'eve y 'media**

...'menos... (to):
2:40= **dos y cua'renta** or **tres 'menos 'veinte**

5:45= **'cinco y cua'renta y 'cinco** or **'seis 'menos cu'arto**

8:57= **'ocho y cincu'enta y si'ete** or **nu'eve 'menos 'tres**

CO'LORES : (Colors)

'rojo/a (red)
a'zul (blue)
ama'rillo/a (yellow)
'blanco/a (white)
'negro/a (black)
'rosa (pink)
na'ranja (orange)
'verde (green)
vio'leta (purple)
gris (gray)
marrón (brown)
bordó (burgundy)
ce'leste (light blue)
do'rado/a (golden)
'plata (silver)
'claro/a (light)
os'curo/a (dark)

As you may know, nowadays there is a wide range of colors with exotic names in the fashion industry. So every season we hear of **'tiza** (chalk), **'vino** (wine), **choco'late** (chocolate), **'guinda** (cherry), **cara'melo** (caramel), **'verde 'agua** (water green), and so on.

Since that is the current trend, you can as

well be original, and ask for **co'lor to'mate** (tomato), or **co'lor acei'tuna** (olive).

TEMPERA'TURA (temperature)

In Argentina we use the Celsius scale, so if you are not familiar with it, you have to remember how to make the conversion :
Formulas :

C = F multiplied by 1.8 + 32

F = C - 32 divided by 1.8

Or, use this quick reference :

 0 C = 32 F
10 C = 50 F
15 C = 60 F
20 C = 70 F
25 C = 78 F
30 C = 87 F
35 C = 91 F

Humidity can be the worst enemy in Buenos Aires, 80% or 90% can turn an innocent summer day into a nightmare. That's why we have a saying that goes : **"Lo que 'mata es la hume'dad."** (It is humidity that kills you).

Listen for the **sensación térmica** (windchill factor), which can also be an unexpected surprise.

20. ADD YOUR OWN PHRASES AND EXPRESSIONS

Word/ Phrase	Meaning/ Traslation	Example

PORTEÑOS TALK

Word/ Phrase	Meaning/ Traslation	Example